Love, Demented

BoundAries

BookLeaf
Publishing

Presentation by *BookLeaf Publishing*

Web: www.bookleafpub.com

E-mail: info@bookleafpub.com

ISBN: 9789358368949

First edition 2023

DEDICATION

Life, liberty, and the pursuit... nah, just life and
a vivid ASS imagination.

ACKNOWLEDGEMENT

Shoutout to God, and all the black moms out there, especially mine. Without either of them, I wouldn't be here.

PREFACE

He wasn't looking through his Third Eye.. Blind.
Smoking that Hoobastank, that made him cough,
sneeze and Blink 182 times.
Cutting coke lines, with his Nine Inch Nails.
There's No Doubt, He will probably end up dead
or in jail.

You

I haven't seen You in awhile, and You never
checked-in.
You rarely answer my calls, so I resort to
texting.
Money can't buy happiness, that is, until I start
spending.
I call You my "You", follow You around and
blend in.

Lost Your scent, You left me on sent.

If I can't have You; then no one can have It.
You cause havoc in traffic, the scene is graphic.
It's tragic, how You handled my heart.
Can't hold a candle to my flame, it's a shame I
couldn't ignite a spark.

She's All That

The moment when I realize that She's the only thing that matters.
When all it takes is a whisper in my ear and I can literally feel my stomach shatter.
Or as soon as Her glance sinks into my eyes, my brain scatters.
Like that of a college student with too much on his platter.
Analytically speaking, if She was the news, I'd be Dan Rather.
If She's Haley, I'm Marshal Mathers.
Even if one day, Her skin wrinkles and She's 50 pounds fatter.
In my world, She'd be the only thing that matters..

Booty Tribute

3

To say Her booty is the motivation, would be an
understatement.
Anywhere one goes, to Her ass, they're adjacent.
Jaws drop in awe, eyes gaze in amazement.
Divine intervention, aligned in perfect
placement.
Designed with grace, from hips to waist.
Eyes green with envy, as their men give chase.
Brace for contact, necks break for a glance.
As they give it all up just for a chance.
"If I had one wish", and hold their hands in
contrition.
Through your thigh gap, all is easy to envision.
With Her ass on a map, cars are still driven with
no ignition.

Bringing Out The Colors In Me

If nothing lasts forever, would She be my
nothing?
Her love is a trampoline, and I'm a kid jumping.
Heartbeat pacing, I'm chasing Her through the
swings, I'm set.
Daydreaming of what an eternity with you
means, yet.

Now I see sounds and hear colors.

Check...Mate

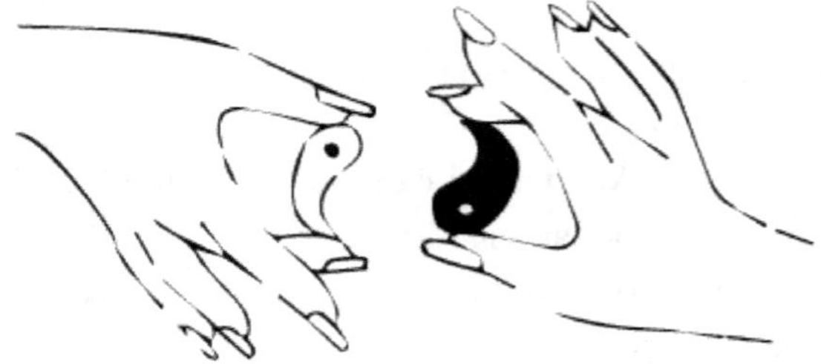

If life is like a chess game, then who's the opponent? And what's life without Her? Nothing, She's the main component..

Muse

Perfection, each time I see You I get lost in Your complexion.
Lose my frame of reference while I count the seconds.
Learn from the lessons, yet I yearn for the connection.
It's the weekend and I can feel it coming like the tension before an election.
For you, did I mention how quickly I would stand at attention?
If it's a war for Your heart, it starts with affection, and never ends on an erection.
If Your love was a tax I would never claim exemption.
Your love takes me to a different dimension.

Save Room, My Love

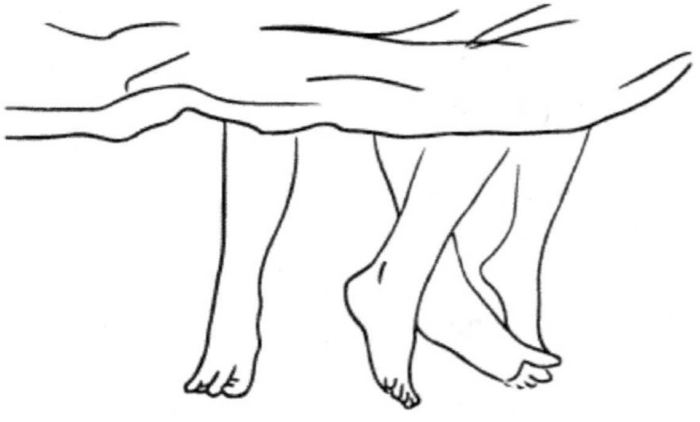

We're not far apart, I can see You in the
distance.
I cherish Your existence.
Kiss your soul when You are in my presence.
Your heart is my home, and I'm the sole tenant.
The definition of love written on our back like
an appendix.

Nostalgic

I'm giddy - just by the epitome of Her essence.

It's a pity - once She departs, I struggle to
complete a sentence.

Heart jumping like I'm running through
adolescence.

Or a kid opening Christmas Day presents.

A fountain of youth, She does much more for
my health than a basket of fruit.

I'm not a businessman, but if She died, I
probably would follow suit.

Cultural Celebration

9

She's mixed, so when I separate Her ass, that's
segregation.
She's equipped, so She demonstrates like a class
in session the whole duration.
Standing at attention, salute, when she blows the
pipe..flute.
Champagne glasses, toast, after She does the
most in the coupe.
Not one to toot my own horn, but the scene was
similar to that of porn, clothes torn, plus She had
the ass to boot.
Scoot, just boogie with me…

Sex Sells

The "P" is never silent, in every sense of the
word.
The way her "P" gets wet, it's truly absurd.
I talk to it, because it listens and I like to be
heard.
She often disturbs the neighbors, while I savor
her taste.
Cater to her needs as I switch pace, no time to
waste.
Leave no trace behind while I'm inside her
space.
A phone call away, She's my safe haven.
Clean-shaven, round of applause as She makes it
clap, standing ovation.

Fallout

Quicksand, why didn't anyone tell me I was
sinking?
I'm seasoned, so this sand is swiftly eating.
Dig my own grave just to put my feet in.
Save every penny I don't see a reason.
Sitting in class, I question what they teaching.
If it ain't about cash, what are you really
seeking?

Love, Rejected

Single people settle down to avoid being lonely.
Love isn't real, there's no emotion you feel.
Love is that dark storm cloud hovering over
your head.
When it rains it pours, the sores on your heart
never heal.
Love is hot, but not the good type, the kind of
hot that makes your skin peel.
Love, at first will have you doing cartwheels and
somersaults.
Week after, we're fighting, playing the blame
game,
I guess it's the summer's fault..

Missed Connection

I miss the love You had for me.

The type of love that would never flee.

Now for Your heart I'd walk to and fro.

Your type of love, I'll never know.

As I roam, I seek a similar version.

Open my heart with teased insertion.

Poison

Secrets taken to the grave held like slaves to your own emotions.
Cyanide, chloride and pesticides, mixed up, call it Genocide's potion.
Drugs are potent, ten capsules of ibuprofen.
Minds deteriorating, you're instigating your brain's corrosion.
The path you've chosen was handwoven.
Like that of grandma's sweater.
Things went sour, starting from the hour you met Her.
Evil addiction, for drugs you scour the world until your soul is devoured.
But the devil is no threat unless you give Him the power.

Fight it..

Unknown Caller

She does me so foul, asks questions with no
answer.

Yet I always seem to dial the right number, but I
only know 6 digits.

Her heart is cold, but for Her I'll expose my soul
to the most frigid.

End my shift by jumping off a cliff to a bed
that's rigid.

As the world spins like a fidget, I sever ties like
burned bridges.

But with Her, I mean business.

I don't control Her, so when angered She's quick
to cruise.

Give me a couple of minutes and I'll prove.

Peel and reveal my heart, black, yet easy to
bruise.

Higher Maintenance

Whether it's Euro, Pound or Yen, all She knows
is to spend.
She texts "daddy" for permission, but forgot to
push send.
She'll expend your assets and may allow access
to Her mattress for the weekend.
She needs keys to the Benz, to buy facial
cleanse.
Magnetic stripe worn out from excessive swipe
trend.
The path to her heart? Before you start, She's a
dead end.
No funds equals no fun.
Unanswered calls, She's "tied up" like loose
ends..

D-Day

You drilled a hole into my back,
As You bore your way to my core,
A tiny spore poured from the bloody shore of
my heart.
Revealed a part of my soul I solely desired to
conceal.
Wholly exposed, can't distinguish a friend from
foe.
Can't extinguish, as the flame grows.
Can't relinquish, for dear life I hold.
Move with urgency, like foot soldiers in
Normandy.

Step on the backs of my ancestors, as they offer
themselves as courtesy.
Reap what you sow, reach your peak with
certainty.
Or die trying..

Worth Behavior

Don't let anyone rob you of your sanity.
Just because your heart throbs, doesn't mean you
should grant amnesty.
Stop wasting your energy, yelling out
obscenities.
Concentrated profanity, get a hold of yourself
and hold you to a higher capacity.
Open your blinds and let the Sun shine on your
vanity.
Because it should be all about you.
The more you argue they continue to
misconstrue the issue.
Take a step back and listen.
Relationships are often more work than you
envision.

One Month

Been about 30 days since we last spoke.
I fell asleep but never woke.
Up all night, your love was a hoax.
Weary, I wear my heart on my sleeve, as she
wears me.
Seek clarity through veracity, find it in a variety
of diamonds, rarity.
Seek security through therapy, moderation is
maturity.
Days bleed together like slit wrist, give my life
like a gift on Christmas.

Now it's day 31…

New Moon

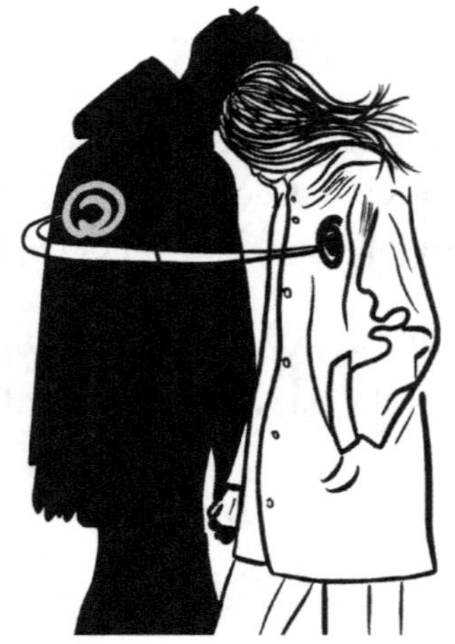

From Venus to Mars, our genus was written in
the stars.
Astronomy to Deuteronomy, coded numerology.
Vision is vivid, as a livid Earth seeks to purge.
If the end is near, we brought it to the verge.

A new moon means a new me.

Tree of Life

Dying on the inside, but thriving on the out.
Stuck in a rut, as you land the dismount. Balance
beam, it seems your wants may outweigh your
dreams.
Co-signer needed to experience the finer things.
Anything that glitters doesn't always glow.
You can plant the seed, but without water, you
won't grow.
Or sun, it looks like you're showing your roots.
Read between the lines and you'll find proof.

9 789358 368949